Property of the Escambia County
~~~~~~

MW01092363

How to Set Up a Classroom for Students with Autism

(A Manual)

By: S. B. Linton
AutismClassroom.com

© 2007 by S. B. Linton. www.autismclassroom.com
All rights reserved.

This book may not be reproduced, stored in a retrieval system, or transmitted by any means electronic, mechanical, photocopying, recording, or otherwise, without written permission from the author.

First Edition: July 2007

Introduction

Welcome to your mentor teacher in a book! This book was written for any teacher, paraprofessional, administrator, related service provider or parent looking to create an effective autism classroom. It is a beginning step to a life long learning process of teaching students with autism. Please understand that there are so many other items that can be discussed in regard to autism and so much more to learn. However, this book is meant to put you on the starting block to creating and running an effective autism classroom. The book is written to be a step by step guide to getting through that first year of teaching students with autism. At the end of the book, you will find a list of several other resources that will further expand your knowledge. This is only a beginning. Congratulations on your purchase and thank you for working with students with autism.

S.B.L.

Table of Contents

Chapter 1

This Is a Process

As you begin your journey to create your spectacular autism classroom, please remember that this is a process. It does take some time and a great deal of energy. It will be worth it in the end. If you are new to teaching, or new to teaching students with autism, you will definitely come across many obstacles along the way which will make you question yourself, your skills, your knowledge and your career choice. However, rest assured, you can do this and you will make it through. If you equip yourself with techniques that you know are appropriate and the consistency to carry those techniques out, you will see the growth in your students over time.

REAL CLASSROOMS:

"It took me a good three months to get my classroom set up the way I wanted it to be. It helped to bring easy stuff home that I could sit in front of the TV and make several nights a week. Then one day projects were completed and the room looked great. I also made some samples and asked our parent volunteer to create the others for the students. She was a tremendous help."

Chapter 2

What You Need to Get Started

There are many, many things needed to set up an autism classroom. I am just going to outline a few. Before you begin, check with your school to see if they already supply the items before you purchase them yourself. The following items will be helpful to you before you start setting up the class:

- 2 boxes of sandwich size zipper baggies
- 2 boxes of gallon zipper baggies
- permanent markers
- Velcro ™ dots (pre-cut) or Velcro ™ strips
- cardstock paper
- foam board
- two 1/2 inch binders for each student
- 2 2-pocket folders for each student
- dividers for binders
- a 3 hole punch device
- clear duct tape
- clear packing tape (to use as a quick laminator)
- self-stick laminating sheets
- depending on your school system—a pack of 8 x 11 inch paper
- white index cards small and large
- 6-12 empty dish pan tubs or bins (dollar store tubs will work)

When thinking about setting up the class, you will also want to "over do it" on the furniture in the classroom. In this case, I feel that "more is more." Having furniture gives you the opportunity to create spaces and boundaries in places where no spaces and boundaries existed. And, since our students need very clear visual boundaries, it is important that we utilize furniture to help us in this process.

Running an effective classroom and getting your needs met also takes some practice in effective communication and the use of good manners. So, *nicely* ask the principal or custodian for some extra desks, chairs and tables, a week or two before school starts. You may not know yet why you need them, however, it is better to have too much furniture and not use it, them to have too little and not be able to really set your classroom up in the manner it needs to be set up. The following furniture ideas may be helpful too:

- student desks, at least 1 per student, unless you are teaching very young students
- tables, various types
- a horseshoe shaped or kidney bean shaped table
- appropriate sized chairs (as many as 3 chairs per student) – you will actually use them all. It will be better to have chair in every area, then to have the students move the chairs from area to area.
- extra filing cabinets or bookshelves
- partitions
- remove teachers and para-professionals desks if you can live without one—they only take up valuable space and give the students something to get into. Besides, while you are teaching all day, you will have no time to ever sit behind a desk!!!

REAL CLASSROOMS:

"I never had a desk. I used a filing cabinet to store my personal belongings. As I looked around the school, some of the best teachers didn't have a desk either or if the desk was there, it was only there to hold up a patrician or it was hidden in some insignificant part of the room."

GAME PLAN:

1. Get a few beginning of the year supplies.

2. Inquire about the type of furniture that is in the classroom you will be using. Ask if it is okay to request any items early, before the school year begins.

Chapter 3

Get To Work Early

If you have the opportunity to go to your school two or three weeks before you are due to report to work for that school year, take the opportunity. Utilize that time to review your student's records, in peace, without all the hustle and bustle of beginning of the school year meetings and in-services. You will need to take about two hours to read all of your student's Individualized Education Plan (IEP) or Individualized Family Service Plan (IFSP) and their educational files. If possible, do this a week or two before school starts. Each Individualized Education Plan has been developed specifically for that child and, as a teacher, you are legally bound to uphold and teach what is on that document. Most often, the IEP document is in a locked area in the school's main office. If you are new, you will need to ask the secretary for the procedure for reading student files. Let her or him know that you are a new teacher and are here to read your student's files. Some schools will require that you keep the document in the locked area, while others will let you read it at a table somewhere in the office. Most often you will have to sign a form show that you read the records. Since you are the case manager, it would be helpful for you to have a copy of the document. Find out what the rules are for your school system regarding this. In order to do this, once again ask the secretary or principal for your copy code or for the process for using the copier. If you are permitted, make a copy of each IEP.

GAME PLAN:

1. Get a full copy of each student's IEP or IFSP.

2. Get a separate copy of the goals and objectives pages for each student.

If you can't get to school a week ahead of time...

If you are starting this process on your first duty day of school, it might be tempting to skip this step and worry about setting up the classroom. However, this is one of the most important items that you need to do. So, if you can, schedule an hour out of the classroom to review your student's files. While you are doing this, you will have classroom team members, the para-professionals in the classroom, who will want to begin preparing the classroom for the students. When you first begin, you might not even know what you want to do, so the pressure of providing guidance to others on what to do to set up the class will be a bit over-whelming. Here are some ideas for classroom team members to work on the first few days before the students return to school:

> *create computer generated name labels for each student (about 6 each)
> *create computer generated name labels for each activity on the schedule
> *make or locate schedule icons for the class daily schedule
> *put up bulletin board paper/ decorate bulletin board
> *create individual student schedules using icons or words
> *make mats or boards for each student to communicate with during mealtimes
> *label zippered baggies with goals and objectives for students, for student work bins
> *label student cubbies or lockers, student chairs, desks or assigned seats, and work bins
> *create a sensory bin for the classroom
> *ask custodians for more furniture or chairs and to remove teacher desk, if needed
> *practice using computer programs for creating picture icons
> *create a reinforcer box or preferred item box for each student
> *label lesson plan bins for each lesson (ex. group reading, math, science, play, etc.)
> *label areas of the classroom
> *make visual supports for self –help skills such as hand-washing, toileting, hanging coat

Chapter 4

Create a Data Collection System

Data Collection is an important tool in measuring the progress students and staff members are making towards IEP or IFSP objectives. Most often, it is more effective to have data taken in the place or activity where the task is performed. This makes it easier to record accurate and reliable data. In your classroom, strive to have all IEP or IFSP objectives tracked regularly through an organized data collection system. The chart below details different types of data.

Types of Data

Frequency- number of times a behavior occurs

Duration- amount of time a behavior occurs

Latency- amount of time between the start of the opportunity and the behavior

Percent- number of occurrences out of the number of opportunities

Intensity- physical force or magnitude of response

Time Sample- observation period divided into intervals

Permanent Product- count of the behavior by observing the product

Interval recording- recording behavior in intervals

Data sheets are needed to record data. There are various types of data sheets which can be used for any given objective. It will be important to locate several types of data sheets so that data can be accurately recorded. For instance, if you want to record the frequency of a student's aggressive behaviors, you may use a data sheet which just allows you to chart tally marks. The tally marks will show you how many times per day that behavior is occurring. To take this data collection idea a little further, if you wanted to know the times that the aggressive behavior is occurring, you may want to use a data sheet which allows for tally marks in a specific time period. Therefore, your data sheet should be more detailed. Examples are below:

Target Behavior: Hitting

///// ///// //

Morning Total= 12

	Hitting	Throwing Items	Biting	Attempted Biting
8:30	///	////		//
9:00	//	/////		//
9:30	///	/////	/	//
10:00	////	///		/
Morning Totals	12	17	1	7

If you are trying to record progress on a task in which the student will be matching, identifying, imitating or labeling to produce a correct response, you may want to use a data sheet which will allow you to record several trials of that same task. This type of data sheet would allow you to:

1. label the individual items the child is focusing on
2. record the child's answer for each trial

Samples of data sheets used for this purpose are below:

The child will point to the correct item when given the label.   ITEM : "SHOE"

DATE	Trial 1	Trial 2	Trial 3	Trial 4	Trial 5	%
5/1						
5/2						
5/3						
5/4						
5/5						

If you choose to use a data sheet such as this, you also may want to have a data sheet for each item the child is to match, identify, imitate or label. Having a separate data sheet is done so that you will know exactly which items on which the child is progressing. However, if you prefer another method, this next data sheet shows how you would highlight specific items on which the student is focusing, on the data sheet.

Objective: The child will point to the correct item, when given the label.

	Trial 1	Trial 2	Trial 3	Trial 4	Trial 5	Total %
Shoe	+	-	-	-	-	20%
Ball	-	+	-	-	+	40%
cookie	-	+	+	+	+	80%
coat	-	-	+	-	-	0%
crayon	-	-	+	+	+	60%

Often, it helps to have several items the student is focusing on listed on one page. This saves time and energy when you are working on a similar task, but are using different items. For example, if the student is supposed to identify colors, you may want a data sheet which allows you to chart the student's progress for three colors on one page. A sample that was shown to me by a mentor is below:

Objective: The student will identify primary colors.

ITEM: "Identify RED"

5/1	5/2	5/3	5/4	5/5
+	-	-	+	-
-	-	-	-	-
+	-	-	+	+
-	-	+	+	+
+	-	+	+	+
3/5	0/5	2/5	4/5	3/5

ITEM: "Identify BLUE"

5/1	5/2	5/3	5/4	5/5
-	-	-	+	-
-	-	-	-	+
-	-	-	+	+
-	-	+	+	+
-	-	+	+	+
0/5	0/5	2/5	4/5	4/5

ITEM: "Identify YELLOW"

5/1	5/2	5/3	5/4	5/5
+	-	+	+	+
+	-	+	+	+
+	-	-	+	+
+	-	+	+	+
+	-	+	+	+
5/5	0/5	4/5	5/5	5/5

Another type of data sheet which is extremely helpful in charting student progress is a task analysis data sheet. This type of data sheet lists all the steps in a task analysis and records the child's progress in each step. A concrete example would be a hand-washing task. During the task of hand-washing, there are several steps that the student must complete. The data sheet for this task would record how well he or she does on each of those steps. In addition, this type of data sheet indicates what type of prompt the student received.

	5/1	5/2	5/3	5/4	5/5				
Turn on Water	P	P	P	P	P				
Get Soap	P	P	P	P	P				
Run water on hands	P	P	P	P	P				
Rub in Soap	P	P	P	P	G				
Put Soap Down	G	G	G	G	I				
Rinse hands under water	P	P	P	P	P				
Turn off Water	P	P	P	P	P				
Get Paper towel	G	G	G	G	V				
Dry Hands	P	P	P	P	P				
Throw paper towel in trash	P	P	G	G	I				

Prompts Needed
I= independent
V=verbal
G= gesture
P=physical assistance

Recording Data...

Anytime you record data or create a data sheet, you want to include the key. The key will tell you how to record the data. In some instances, you may only want to know if the student was correct or incorrect. In other instances, you may want to know the prompt level the student received to complete the task. In either case, always include the key on any data sheets to be used in the classroom.

KEY
I= independent
V=verbal
G= gesture
P=physical assistance

KEY
+ = correct
- = incorrect
NR = no response

Permanent product data sheets are data sheets in which the student's actual production of the task is right there on the paper. This type of data sheet or "work sample" allows you to actually see what the student can produce. Permanent product data sheets can be useful for documenting writing skills, tracing skills and coloring skills. If a student's objective is to color within a circle 4 out of 5 times, you could create a data sheet which has 5 circles and have the student color inside them. As they complete the task you write directly on the paper the prompt level the student needed to complete the task. A sample of the data sheet is below:

Color in the Circles.

As you may see, even in these few examples, there are many ways to create data sheets. You will need to create and use data sheets which are meaningful to you, since you will be the person interpreting the data and reporting the student progress to the parents. Also, remember that the objectives can be handwritten on the data sheets or cut and pasted, depending upon what is easiest. Regardless of what type of data sheets you choose to use, just know that it is extremely important to start now and create the data sheets first. Having data sheets helps to organize and focus your teaching. They do so by showing you exactly what skills to focus in on during your lessons.

GAME PLAN:

1. Get a copy of each student's goals and objectives.

2. Have a binder for each student's objectives.

3. Make enough copies of several types of blank data sheets to get started.

4. Make a data sheet for each objective.

5. Organize the data sheets for specific centers and activities in a binder or folder for each student. For an added bonus, place the student's individual schedule on the front of the binder. This way they bring the data sheets to you as they travel from activity to activity.

6. Organize "all day" data sheets such as those for communication, toileting and behavior on a clipboard or up hang them up on the wall.

Things to Think About When Creating Data Systems:

- Remember that this process will take about 2 hours.
- Make enough blank copies of various types of data sheets before beginning.
- You will need to first have a copy of each child's IEP in a binder or folder in your possession for you to access easily.
- An individualized binder or folder which holds each child's data sheets is also needed for each student.
- Make two copies of each student's goals and objectives. Use one copy to cut and paste the objectives from the IEP or IFSP onto the data sheets, instead of using time rewriting the objective. If you choose to write the objectives on the data sheets, that can work too. Do this for each student's objectives. You will have one data sheet per objective.
- With the other copy of goals and objectives, use it to write down (next to the objective) the category under which that objective falls. For instance, if the objective says that the student will read sight words, then you know that that task is in the "reading" category. The goal is that by the end of this process, you will have a data sheet for every objective *and* a plan for what types of categories or activities will be needed in your classroom.
- While reviewing the goals and objectives, you are also sorting them into categories according to the type of objective. Be sure to write them next to the objective. Some suggestions for category names include, but are not limited to: 1:1 IEP tasks, reading tasks, math tasks, play/socialization tasks, cognitive tasks, communication objectives, behavior objectives, independent work objectives, and self-help objectives (ex. hand-washing, toileting, hanging book bag, etc.) These examples were chosen because most goals and objectives fit into one of these categories.
- After you determine the categories, then turn the categories into activities that you will include in your daily schedule. By labeling the objective, a clear view of the types of activities you need to have should be obtained. For example, if you have 6 students with fine motor objectives, then you clearly need to have a fine motor activity in your schedule. Keep in mind that some objectives may overlap in various activities. Although you might choose to practice the skill in both areas, you may choose to keep data in only one area. Examples of activities for data collection opportunities might be morning routine, opening, reading center, math center, fine motor, cognitive tasks, 1:1 work, structured play, mealtimes, large group activities, snack, all day data collection (ex. behavior, communication, etc.).
- Discuss data collection as a team. Make sure that all staff know how to record the data accurately and are using the same key/symbols. Also, make sure that all staff members use the same verbal direction when asking the child to perform the objective. It sometimes helps to write down on the data sheet exactly what the staff member should say to get the student to perform the task.
- Data should be taken in the area where the activity/task is performed.

Chapter 5

Schedules are the Key to Stress Relief

Adults use schedules, calendars, checklists and appointment books to keep track of appointments and events. For many adults, these visual supports help them to organize their lives and clarify where and when they are to participate in those various events. Visual schedules also help students with autism. They do so by helping the student to clarify what events or activities will occur during that school day. Other types of schedules may tell the student what will occur in each activity or help indicate when an activity will end. Schedules often assist in reducing anxiety for students with autism and help promote further independence in student functioning. Visual schedules are a necessary and essential component of any classroom that serves students with autism. If adults require written, visual schedules to help monitor their lives, remember what an especially important function these schedules play in the daily movements of students with autism.

There are several types of schedules needed in an autism classroom:

1. Classroom Weekly Schedule
2. Student's Individual/Personal Schedule
3. Daily Class Schedule
4. Task or Mini-task Schedule
5. Reinforcement Schedule
6. Staff Breaks and Lunch Breaks Schedule

Classroom Weekly Schedule

Creating a good, appropriate and accurate classroom weekly schedule is a critical part of running an effective autism classroom program. This is your next step in the process. Committing to the schedule and doing what is listed on the schedule is extremely important for the students. So, when you create the schedule, be sure to include those items that may actually happen during that school day and allow a sufficient enough amount of time for those activities. There are several factors to consider that can help you create a good, appropriate, schedule.

Things to consider when developing a CLASSROOM WEEKLY SCHEDULE:

- **Development**- Develop the schedule first, then arrange the room to fit the activities you placed in the schedule.
- **Use Pencil**- You will change the schedule several times.
- **Timing**- Generally a good amount of time for activities is 15-20 minutes, allowing 5 or so minutes extra for transition.
- **Activity Names**- Give each area/activity its own name (www.teacch.com). Each area of the class or activity should, when possible, have its own name so that students are clear about what they are expected to do and where they are expected to go. Don't forget to add bathroom breaks!
- **Routines and Sequencing**- Establish and develop consistent routines the students can count on. This will assist in the student's ability to become independent and increase positive behavior in that activity. The schedule should have consistent routines that occur in the same order as much as possible. The timing of these activities is not as important as the sequencing of the activities. Also, activities should occur in the same area each time. If the art activity is at the round table on Tuesday, it should not be at the square table on Wednesday. If possible, ask specialists to consider making the specials for your class occur at the same time slot each day so the students will know that at this time slot, they always go out of the room to a special activity.
- **Movement**- Remember the students need to move around and engage in exercise when scheduling time allotments for activities. Try to vary standing up and sitting down activities. For example, can a pre-scheduled walk to the hall bathroom offer a much needed exercise break for a student who has trouble sitting for a long time? Also, consider student movement in between activities within the classroom. Will the order of your activities make for a smooth transition if students have to pass the snack tray or an open door before getting to the work table? Avoid having the students stay in the same area for too many activities.
- **Groupings**- Consider grouping those students with objectives that are similar. The objectives will help to determine patterns in the student's programs. These patterns can help to tell what areas or activities will need to be taught in the classroom. Decide which students will be in small groups together while developing the schedule. Pay special attention to what students work well together, what students do not work well together, what students have similar objectives or what students have similar learning styles.
- **Small Group Centers Schedules**- Develop a separate schedule for your small group centers that *indicates what students will be at each small group center/station, when they will be there and where the center is located*. Make it very clear. Post it on the wall.
- **Post It**- Sometimes it helps to have several copies of this schedule around the room, to serve as a visual prompt for staff members.

Sample Weekly Schedule

	Monday	Tuesday	Wednesday	Thursday	Friday
8:00	Morning Activity Box & Bathroom	Morning Activity Box & Bathroom	Morning Activity Box & Bathroom	Morning Activity Box & Bathroom	Morning Activity Box & Bathroom
8:15	Breakfast	Breakfast	Breakfast	Breakfast	Breakfast
8:30	Opening (Circle Time)	Opening (Circle Time)	Opening (Circle Time)	Opening (Circle Time)	Opening (Circle Time)
8:45	Opening (Circle Time)	Opening (Circle Time)	Opening (Circle Time)	Opening (Circle Time)	Opening (Circle Time)
9:00	Group Reading	Speech Time	Group Reading	Group Reading	Group Reading
9:15	Group Reading	Speech Time	Group Reading	Group Reading	Group Reading
9:30	Centers (IEP Reading Objectives, Structured Play, Writing/ Fine Motor)	Centers (IEP Reading Objectives, Structured Play, Writing/ Fine Motor)	Centers (IEP Reading Objectives, Structured Play, Writing/ Fine Motor)	Centers (IEP Reading Objectives, Structured Play, Writing/ Fine Motor)	Centers (IEP Reading Objectives, Structured Play, Writing/ Fine Motor)
9:45	Centers (con't)	Centers (con't)	Centers (con't)	Centers (con't)	Centers (con't)
10:00	Centers (con't)	Centers (con't)	Centers (con't)	Centers (con't)	Centers (con't)
10:15	Centers (con't)	Centers (con't)	Centers (con't)	Centers (con't)	Centers (con't)
10:30	Centers (con't)	Centers (con't)	Centers (con't)	Centers (con't)	Centers (con't)
10:45	Bathroom & Exercise Movement	Bathroom & Exercise Movement	Bathroom & Exercise Movement	Bathroom & Exercise Movement	Bathroom & Exercise Movement
11:00	Lunch	Lunch	Lunch	Lunch	Lunch
11:15	Lunch	Lunch	Lunch	Lunch	Lunch
11:30	Structured Recess	Community Trip	Structured Recess	Structured Recess	Structured Recess
11:45	Sensory Table & Bathroom	Community Trip	Sensory Table & Bathroom	Sensory Table & Bathroom	Sensory Table & Bathroom
12:00	Motor	Community Trip	OT	Motor	Art or Music
12:15	Motor	Community Trip	OT	Motor	Art or Music
12:30	Independent Work	Community Trip	Speech Time	Independent Work	Independent Work
12:45	Independent Work	Community Trip	Speech Time	Independent Work	Independent Work
1:00	Group Math	Group Math	Group Math	Group Math	Group Math
1:15	Math Centers	Math Centers	Math Centers	Math Centers	Math Centers
1:30	Snack	Snack	Snack	Snack	Snack
1:45	Storytime & Bathroom	Storytime & Bathroom	Storytime & Bathroom	Storytime & Bathroom	Storytime & Bathroom
2:00	Closing & Pack Up	Closing & Pack Up	Closing & Pack Up	Closing & Pack Up	Closing & Pack Up
2:15	Dismissal	Dismissal	Dismissal	Dismissal	Dismissal

Blank Weekly Schedule

	Monday	Tuesday	Wednesday	Thursday	Friday
8:00					
8:15					
8:30					
8:45					
9:00					
9:15					
9:30					
9:45					
10:00					
10:15					
10:30					
10:45					
11:00					
11:15					
11:30					
11:45					
12:00					
12:15					
12:30					
12:45					
1:00					
1:15					
1:30					
1:45					
2:00					
2:15					

REAL CLASSROOMS:

"My first week or two of school was spent just getting through the schedule. Sometimes after the transition to the activity, even if the students were only in the activity for 5 minutes I was happy. What I figured, was that by doing that, I was allowing them to get used to the routine. That was worth its weight in gold! It is so temping to just change the plan and do something easier, but easier doesn't cut it in the long run. Any new teacher should remember that the first week or so, activities will take more time to accomplish because every routine will be new to them and the students. It is okay to invest that time now. The kids will catch on."

Scheduling Related Services:

Try to find the Related Service Providers on the first day -- before they make their schedules. Ask to have your specials in the afternoon, if possible. This way, you will have the coverage you need when the classroom staff takes lunch breaks. Some specialists may not be able to do this, but it is worth a try.

Daily class schedule

The daily class schedule is the schedule which tells what activities will occur that particular school day. The daily class schedule should be posted on the board each day using some type of adhesive such as Velcro™ or magnet tape. This type of schedule should be easy for students to follow and should be large enough to see from across the room. You will want to go back to the schedule in between activities to show the students that each activity is finished and what activity will be occurring next. The type of schedule used will depend on your student's ability levels and receptive language skills. For some classes, this daily class schedule will consist of objects, for some it may have only pictures, and yet, for others, it might be accompanied by written words. In any case, the schedule should be an *accurate* account of what is to be expected that day. Many students will be counting on the visual schedule to let them know what is happening that day. The daily schedule can be placed in a horizontal or vertical position. To limit distraction to students and increase their ability to read the schedule, the area around the visually-based daily classroom schedule, should be free of clutter.

Individual/personal schedule

Individual or personal student schedules can take many forms. They are needed to help students organize and learn routines. In addition, they can help some students tolerate changes in routine. Individual student schedules build predictability in to the lives of students with autism and may relieve stress for other students with autism by giving them an idea of what to expect. Many students will begin to develop independent skills for monitoring their daily activities by using schedules. Individual student schedules are beneficial for students who have a difficult time dealing with changes to a routine. They also can be helpful in identifying activities that may be distinct to that particular student. For example, if you have a student who needs more break times than others, then his personal schedule will show more break times than the regular class schedule. A personal schedule might also show sensory input activities which are specific to that student, individual speech therapy times, small group areas, or toileting opportunities, which may not be the same exact time as the other students.

Please understand that these schedules may take some time to develop. You will first have to see several types of schedules to know which type you like or which type you feel will be appropriate for your students. AutismClassroom.com has some links to sample schedules on the "Set Up an Autism Class" page. Try providing yourself or your classroom team members with a time line in which you aim to have the individual schedules created for each student. If it is easier, try only concentrating on creating two individual schedules a week, until all are finished. The following page offers a sample of what the daily class schedule may look like for a particular day and what the individualized/personal schedule may look like for one student. You will notice that the same activities are on both, but the individualized schedule gives the student greater detail related to the things he can expect to have happen that day. For example, it shows him which centers he will be going to and in what order.

Weekly Class Schedule	**Individual/Personal Schedule with scheduled break times**
Opening Reading Centers Clean-up Sensory time Lunch Recess Math Seatwork Art Snack Clean Up Closing	Opening Walk Reading Lotion Break Play Center Work Center Fine Motor Center Clean-up Sensory time Lunch Recess Weighted Vest Math Sensory Brush Seatwork Walk Art Snack Clean Up(Stack chairs) Closing

One key similarity in all individual schedules is that they all have a finished component, in which the student symbolizes that an activity is completed. As my mentor advised me, students *need to be taught how* to use their schedules. They may require most-to-least prompting and physical guidance for a while. Individual student schedules are made to fit the specific needs and abilities of the students and would use real objects, pictures, icons or words depending on what the child can relate to. The schedules should be available to students for use throughout the school day.

REAL CLASSROOMS:

"I had to teach each child to use his personal schedule. It took a long time. Some students caught on to the concept and for others, it was difficult conceptually. Three became independent in using it and the others would look at the pictures or move the picture when we asked them to do it."

<u>Task schedule</u>

Task schedules, also called mini- task schedules (Hodgdon, 1995) could be thought of as directions. They help to visually "break down" a task or an activity for a student. Task schedules show a student what will occur within the context of a structured lesson or activity, much like directions. Task schedules can also help students perform tasks without the use of a verbal prompt from the adult, thus increasing independence. They are used to give students a visual cue of what is expected. Task schedules are helpful throughout the day. They also should be created based on the child's ability level and they will take time to create. To start with, you may want to create task schedules for routine activities that you have frequently such as, reading, math, opening, play time and work time. The task schedule could to be made using a sturdy board, like foam board or cardstock and have detachable icons, photos or objects. If it is an activity that will occur infrequently, it is sometimes easier to make a quick task schedule on a piece of paper or index card, which is specific to an activity or task that will be occurring only once.

Icons Which Could be Used on Task Schedules for Activities...

Opening	Reading	Work	Clean Table
Names	book	work	pick up sponge
Day	turn page	play	turn on water
Months	read	help	wet sponge
Numbers	paper	finished	wipe table
Calendar	listen		rinse sponge
Schedule	work		put sponge away
Song	pictures		

Independent Work Schedules

Independent Work Schedules help students to manage their time. They are used to promote independent task completion and to decrease student need for adult intervention. These types of schedules tell students exactly what work activity is required of them during independent work, how much they are responsible for completing and when they will be finished. Independent work schedules can be created in many different ways. These visual schedules should be sure to indicate any break times during the independent work session. Independent work schedules should include a finished component so that students can indicate when their work is complete. The book Activity Schedules for Children with Autism by McClannahan &. Krantz (1998) offers many good examples and detailed strategies for creating work or activity schedules. Ideas and more information for independent work tasks can be found in chapter 6 of this book.

Student Break Schedule (when needed)

Student break/reinforcement schedules give students a visual indicator of when their reinforcement, preferred item, or break will occur. These may be helpful for a child who is on a behavior intervention plan and needs to be reminded that their reinforcement will be coming soon. The visual support, without the teacher needing to verbally relay that message, is helpful.

Staff Breaks and Lunch Schedules

This topic is an easy one to overlook. However, having a set plan for when adults will be out of the room is critical for implementing any classroom program. What you will find, is that there are simply some things you cannot do without your full team. To be safe, it is best to have at least two people in the room at all times. So what you have to do is schedule activities that can be easily managed by less people during team members break times and lunch times. In addition to this, it will be critical that all staff members realize that all hands will be needed during non-break times. Some teachers opt not to take a lunch break, but I strongly encourage you to take some time out of the room each day since this is a challenging occupation.

A good way to tackle this task is to look on your weekly class schedule and identify three ½ hour blocks which appear to be okay times for staff members to take their lunch breaks. Be sure to check if the activities during that time period can be conducted with a staff member out of the room. For example, a reading lesson would probably not work during a time when a staff member is out of the room. However, a sensory activity, which most of the students will find motivating, will be easy to conduct with a staff member out of the room. After you have identified the ½ hour time slots, have each team member sign up for a lunch time and stick to it. Try the same method for any short breaks times too. Doing so will make for better organization and efficiency in the classroom.

GAME PLAN:

1. Ask if specialists can give you afternoon specials.

2. Create a tentative weekly schedule- in pencil.

3. You or a team member, make or find picture representations or object representations of each activity in your schedule and laminate.

4. Put up the schedule for the next day of school.

5. Investigate types of individual student schedules to see what you like. Create them and laminate.

Chapter 6

Effective Classroom Set Up

After the weekly class schedule has been created, it will be necessary for you to create a successful classroom set-up that is designed specifically for students with autism. The use of furniture, carpet, carpet pieces, bookshelves, desks, and much, much more can be utilized to the advantage of you, the "classroom designer." As a "classroom designer" you and your team will need to think just as that, a designer, who will systematically mix functional work spaces, efficient data collection systems, visual supports, individualized materials, and organized routines and procedures, to create and sustain an effective autism classroom. The ideas for some of the various elements included in this chapter came from a private school's classroom checklist that I read 10 years ago and the information has stuck with me and has been priceless. It is extremely important information for any teacher beginning to set up your classroom. The rest of this chapter is intended to describe those elements needed in each classroom with a little more explanation. The areas of Setting, Keeping Students Focused, Visual Strategies for Expressing and Receiving Language, Student Centered Planning, and Organizing All of the Pieces are included.

Setting

Since students with autism tend to be visual learners, it is important for the design of the classroom to exhibit clear visual boundaries (www.TEACCH.com). This will help students who may have a difficult time establishing their own boundaries by creating parameters by which they can function. The physical design of the class should make certain that the first activity is easy for students to get to. In addition, the student's space should be clearly defined either with a photo or the child's name. Photos, picture icons or written words posted around the room that indicate the names of various areas and activities of the classroom are a necessity for helping students, who are visual learners, to navigate through their environment. The "classroom designer" will also need to make sure that the data collection system is systematically in or near each area where data will need to be collected. Sometimes folders and binders help with this.

The physical design of the classroom will also consist of the various areas of the classroom. Areas of the classroom should be specific and used for one activity only, when possible (www.TEACCH.com). When you are setting up the room, be sure to include the following areas which tend to work well in most autism classrooms:

-Independent work stations: In this area, students will work on structured work tasks by themselves (eventually) from start to finish. At first they may need much guidance from you. This space tends to be more beneficial if each student should has their own desk or work space and their own set of materials. Creating materials for this area may take some time. If you start with one or two sets of materials for each student, you can build upon it later. Independent work tasks need to be tasks that the student is already skilled at doing. The goal is to get the students to work for an extended period of time, not to learn a new skill. Tasks should be related to the IEP objectives and they should be easy to look at, understand and complete, without help from the adult. Typically, the tasks should be set up to be completed in a left to right or top to bottom sequence (www.TEACCH.com). After completing work tasks, the students will need a place to store their finished work. This tends to be a place to the right of the student, such as an empty box or container, which symbolizes that a task is finished. The University of North Carolina's TEACCH program utilizes jigs (structured work tasks) for teaching independent work. Some really good examples of these work tasks can be found at AutismClassroom.com on the "Classroom Organization" page.

Independent Work Tasks Area
Tips for Implementation

- These particular work tasks will be hands on activities designed to have the student learn to be productive and independent. They will be different from teacher directed lessons that teach new concepts. These tasks will reinforce known concepts.
- Select an area of the room where students can be monitored easily during the activity. Possibly place desks against the wall and have students face the wall for less distractions.
- Collect various containers or ask parents to send in containers of various sizes with lids.
- Velcro ™ works well for keeping materials grounded.
- Large storage bins can help to hold each child's work tasks.
- Photo or icons of the tasks may help to show each student which work task they are to complete.
- Use an icon to show "finished" or "reinforcer" when done.
- Start with having the students complete one small task, then provide them with a reinforcer item or toy. Gradually work up to adding more tasks.
- Provide only physical prompts, no verbal comments for completing the work tasks, since the goal is to get them to complete the task without the verbal prompting from the adult. Gradually decrease the physical prompts as time goes on (McClannahan &. Krantz, 1998). The Activity Schedules book by McClannahan &. Krantz, provides more information on this topic.

-1:1 or 2:1 work areas: Direct instruction of IEP objectives provided by the teacher or para-professional should take place in the work area. Two or three work areas which each provide direct instruction of IEP objects can be occurring at one time. Try to make these areas separated from the large group area. Use this method only if this works for your students. Some classrooms find they have to set up a system where only one student is pulled at a time for direct instruction. In either case, in order to promote efficiency in instruction, each member of your classroom team must be aware of their assigned station and the materials should be ready and in place in that area before the lesson begins. Classroom teachers

should be sure to review each child's IEP objectives and data collection system with all classroom staff members to be sure everyone is on the same page.

1:1 or 2:1 Work Area
Tips for Implementation

- Zipper-type baggies are helpful for storing each child's individual materials and reinforcers. Try purchasing several sizes from extra small to jumbo. They will always come in handy.
- Create one labeled baggie for each objective the student can work on in a 1:1 desk top setting. (For example, bathroom goals or mealtime objectives would not fit in to this category. However, matching, sorting and identifying items may work well in this area.) Store the materials for each objective in their own baggie. Use a permanent marker to write on the baggie.
- A reinforcer box or container for each child which has a variety of about 6 or 7 reinforcers or preferred items chosen specifically for that child will be useful. These selected reinforcers will be most effective if students are only allowed access to them during work times and not at other times.
- Limit distractions by selecting work areas near a blank wall or in areas with limited visual distractions (www.TEACCH.com). If there is not blank wall, place bulletin board paper, plain fabric or foam board up to create a blank space.
- Dividers for work areas can be made with PVC piping and fabric, bookshelves, patricians, large pieces of cardboard or any other pieces of furniture that are sturdy and cannot hurt someone if knocked down.

REAL CLASSROOMS:

"After about one week the work bins were completed with the materials inside. It made it so easy. I didn't have to think about lesson plans during work time—the IEP objectives were the lesson and the materials were already in the bin! Setting up like this did make reporting student progress easier too. Most of the data was taken every day when we worked on the materials in the work bins."

Discrete Trial Teaching (DTT)...

Discrete Trial Teaching (DTT) is a one of several popular strategies used when working with young children with autism. Sometimes you will hear it referred to as ABA or Applied Behavior Analysis, but their definitions are actually different. This is **just one** technique in a **variety** of available teaching methods you can use as a teacher of students with autism. DTT is described as common intervention used to shape a young child's behavior and to teach which involves a three-part process: a presentation by a teacher; the child's response; and a consequence (www.iancommunity.org). A particular trial may be repeated several times in succession, several times a day, over several days (or even longer) until the skill is mastered (www.polyxo.com). The strategy includes the breaking down of tasks in to minute pieces in order to create correct responses.

DTT works well with 1 to 1 teaching time because you can concentrate on one task with one student. An example of a task where you may use discrete trial teaching would be if a student was to identify primary colors. Instead of presenting all of the colors at once and you would present maybe two colors and have the student choose one. You would "drill" this one color concept several times, before moving on to the next one. In addition to the presentation of the task, you would provide preferred items that the child likes, when they produce a correct answer. More information on Discrete Trial Teaching can be found in the following books:

Teaching Individuals with Developmental Delays: Basics Intervention Techniques, by I. Lovaas

A Work in Progress: Behavior Management Strategies and a Curriculum for Intensive Behavioral Treatment of Autism, by Leaf, Boehm, Harsh, & McEachin

Behavioral Intervention For Young Children with Autism: A Manual for Parents and Professionals, by Maurice, Green, & Luce.

-Sensory-motor area/space: The sensory-motor area is a space for students to unwind and receive the sensory input they may need to focus, calm and organize themselves. The sensory-motor space may include, but is not limited to, activities or items such as a large therapy balls, tunnels, pillows, lotions, bubbles, brushes, a sand table, and other large motor movement equipment. Collaboration with Occupational Therapists is essential to providing help in planning for this area.

Sensory Motor Area /Space
Tips for Implementation

- Talk with the Occupational Therapist regarding sensory needs for each student. Perhaps they can guide you to, or provide you with, information on sensory differences in students with autism.
- Create a space to store the items when not in use.
- All team members will need to be involved with the implementation of this activity.
- Let the student guide you to the items they like.
- Have fun with the students during this activity.
- Children's music with an upbeat tempo or calming music, can help, depending on what mood you want to create.
- Eventually build communication into this activity by having the students indicate to you which item they would like to have. They can do this by asking, signing or giving a picture of the item. If you have a closet, the pictures can be stored on the closet and the equipment inside. Then students will have to give you the picture or ask for it, in order to get the item.

-Structured Play/Rec-Leisure Area: The play area may look different in every room. You have to create it to meet your student's needs. Most often, for younger students, the play area will need to be sectioned off with very clear boundaries. For older students, some classroom teams choose to create a table at which the students can play games or cards or participate in some other

recreation/leisure activity. In the play area, the use of topic boards, age-appropriate activities, and emphasis on communication and socialization skills should be taught. Play/leisure activities should be structured, planned and guided by the adults. For students with autism, direct instruction of rec/leisure and play skills is critical for their social development.

Structured Play/Rec-Leisure Area
Tips for Implementation

- Play time is not break time.
- Remember you will have to teach play skills. They do not come naturally for some students with autism.
- Teach the play skills 1:1 first, then incorporate them into a group setting (Moyes, 1997).
- Use age appropriate games and toys to the extent possible. If a typically developing seven year old likes the game, chances are, your seven year old you are working with will have some interest in it too. You may just have to modify the presentation a little.
- Find a way to make the game or activity "do-able" for the student.
- Have fun. The students should want to come to this area of your room. If you are not having fun, they are not having fun.
- If you are going to play, then play. Do not drill the student on colors and shapes and numbers, etc. during the play time. It is okay to comment on these concepts, but keep the play fun and engaging and the opposite of work time.
- Teach the skills they need. You are the facilitator. Do not leave them to "play on their own."
- Read up on teaching play skills to students with autism. It can be an education within itself, since there is so much to learn.

-*Small Group Areas (centers/stations):* Dividing students into small groups tends to improve their level of concentration. Stations/centers can be used to do this. Each center/station should serve a purpose. For example, a fine motor station, a 2:1 or 1:1 work station and a structured play station may work well to address IEP objectives in those areas, for elementary aged students. For secondary level students, the centers/stations might consist of a survivals skills or social skills station, math station, and reading skills station. Still others may choose to have 3 centers of work time occurring at once. It is up to you to find out what works for your students. Within each station, a system for keeping data on that student's IEP objective needs to be present and the data should be recorded immediately.

Small Group Areas (centers/stations)
Tips for Implementation

- All team members should be in the room when conducting small groups. It is a good idea to schedule staff breaks at a different time.
- Create a schedule to identify which students will be at which station/center. After 15-20 minutes, the students can rotate to the next center/station. It often helps to have the students rotate in the same direction each time, so they are not confused.
- The adults in the class will need to know which center they will be responsible for teaching. They will need a schedule too. You can decide if each adult will keep the same center/station for a week or for the year.
- If you have any group with three students, you will need three seats in every center.
- Extra reinforcer boxes come in handy during this activity for those students who may need to wait. Have a box or zippered baggie full at each center, if needed.

Centers/ Stations ...

The first week you try this it will be hectic and difficult. Just stick through it and rearrange furniture, students, or staff members until you get a system that works. You will also have some students that may not want to cooperate or may exhibit challenging behaviors. Be sure not to let their challenging behaviors excuse them from the work that they are in school to do. Sometimes you might need to give the student with challenging behaviors a preferred item (that can be used at the table) just for coming to the center. For a few days, you may just be working on getting them to sit in the area, even if it means them playing with that preferred item. So you may have to let them use their preferred item for a while and then have him or her do one very small work task, then you give the item back. Each subsequent work session you will increase the amount of work. After a while, you will then have him/her do two tasks, then a break/preferred item, then three tasks and a break/preferred item, etc.

Sample Small Groups/Centers Schedule

Sample #1 with groups of 2 students.

Time	FINE MOTOR IEP WORK	READING IEP WORK	STRUCTURED PLAY
9:00-9:30	1st Sara & John	1st Sam & Colin	1st Trina & Eduardo
9:30-10:00	2nd Trina & Eduardo	2nd Sara & John	2nd Sam & Colin
10:00-10:30	3rd Sam & Colin	3rd Trina & Eduardo	3rd Sara & John

Sample #2 with 1:1 time for each student and group time for the others. This sample requires 4 adults in the classroom.

Time	1:1 with Sue	1:1 with Jen	Group Activity w/ Mitch and Tina
9:00-9:30	1st -1:1 TIME Sara	1st -1:1 TIME Sam	1st –PLAY TIME John Colin Trina Eduardo
9:30-10:00	2nd -1:1 TIME John	2nd -1:1 TIME Colin	2nd –FINE MOTOR Sara Sam Trina Eduardo
10:00-10:30	3rd -1:1 TIME Trina	3rd -1:1 TIME Eduardo	3rd – SENSORY TABLE Sara Sam John Colin

Sample #3 with afternoon 1:1 time for 3 students and small group activities for the other students (assuming the other 3 students had 1:1 time in the morning).

Time			
12:00-12:30	1st **1:1 Time** Sam	1st **Independent Work Area** Sara & John	1st **Sensory Area** Colin, Trina & Ed
12:30-1:00	2nd **1:1 Time** Colin	2nd **Independent Work Area** Trina, Ed & Sam	2nd **Sensory Area** Sara & John
1:00-1:30	3rd **1:1 Time** Ed	3rd **Story Group** Sara, Colin, Sam Trina & John	3rd **Story Group** Sara, Colin, Sam Trina & John

-Large Group Lesson Area: The large group lesson area should be an area with a table with enough space to accommodate all students. It may be helpful to decide in advance the student seating arrangement. This further helps to promote predictability and routine in the student's programming. If you have a student who runs or darts away, it may be helpful to be sure that the student sits with their back facing a wall or divider and the adult sits facing the student, between the student and the door. For some classrooms, horseshoe-shaped tables offer a more effective method for interacting with students during the large group lesson.

Large Group Area
Tips for Implementation

- Create a labeled bin for each large group lesson (even snack time).
- Put all materials in the bin for the next lesson.
- After each lesson, (after school or at the end of the day) remove all material except for the next lesson's materials.
- During the lessons, model what you wan the students to do. Always make an extra so that you can first show them how to do it, and then have them imitate what you did.
- The more hands on the activity, the more likely the students will be to participate and pay attention. Try to include real items with each of your lessons, as well as pictures. For example, if you are doing a lesson on going on a vacation, bring in a suitcase and real items that you might pack in it as part of your lesson. The students will respond to real items in addition to the pictures of the items.
- Have a visual topic board to show the students what you will discuss during the lesson. It can be used as a review when the lesson is finished. A laminated piece of card stock paper could be used for this or a piece of foam board, with Velcro™ attached, works well for this.
- Clipboards often help for storing communication objectives or data sheets for each student. They provide easy access to the information and data sheets during group lessons.
- Have student's backs face a wall or divider. If their backs face the open classroom, they have a greater chance of leaving the table or leaving the area.

Do a walk through...

After you have set up the physical space in your room, but before the students arrive, try a "walk through" the classroom as a student on the first day. Take your schedule and see what the students would do in each activity from the beginning of the day until the end. The walk through should help you sort out any inconsistencies in your planning. It will also help you to see if you have the materials ready for the first day. Be sure to include some extra activities incase the student's therapy sessions or specials/creative arts activities do not start up right away on the first day.

Keeping Students Focused

Due to the student's tendency to be easily distracted, you want to be sure to have low distraction levels in your classroom. This includes visual distractions such as hanging items and auditory distractions such as music playing during instructional times. Another distracting thing that some people tend to forget is the movement of chairs from one area of the room to the next. If at all possible, try to get enough chairs so that they are in each place you need them. This will eliminate the need to move them around the room during instructional time. If appliances are distracting, they should be removed, placed out of reach or covered. When choosing colors for a bulletin board, try using calming colors such as blue or green, instead of colors which could be alerting for some people, such as red, orange or yellow. Also, I have seen some classroom teams use a solid color fabric (similar to a curtain) to cover shelves that are distracting to students.

Students That Run, Elope & Dart...

Whatever you want to call them, their game plan is still the same. They want to run, run, run and run. This can be extremely scary and dangerous in a classroom or school building. If you have a student who runs without notice, you may find yourself on edge a lot more than you had hoped to be. Please find out before the school year starts if the student has a history of running from the adult. Although this behavior is challenging, there are a few tricks you can put up your sleeve to TRY to eliminate this behavior:

-childproof locks on the doorknobs of the classroom

-use furniture as a natural barrier for various areas of the classroom

-if the student is seated and you are seated behind him or her, place your feet on the bottom of the legs of the chair so that the chair cannot move back

-seat the student in the middle of the group so that if he or she gets up, the others create a natural barrier, which will just give you a little more time to react

-do not respond verbally to the student's running. Go as quickly as you can to get the student and bring them back to the activity. Only talk about the activity they are supposed to do, do **not** talk about the behavior that is inappropriate. But try your best not to encourage the behavior by saying "Bad job" or "Stop running" or "No." Many times this verbal reinforcement is exactly what the student wants you to do. (You can tell by the smile on their face when you say it!)

Visual Strategies for Expressing and Receiving Language

Visual strategies of several types are needed to help students with autism in an effectively run autism classroom. Visual supports include any visual item that helps a child to understand or express language. They include, but are not limited to photo icons, calendars, schedules, topic boards, single icons, written lists, written words, logos, and more.

-*Visual Schedules:* Visual student schedules are made to fit the specific needs of the students (i.e. object, picture icon, photo, word). These schedules should be available to students for use throughout the school day. Student schedules are made in a variety of ways and based on the needs of the student. Chapter 5 describes types of schedules in detail.

-*Augmentative Communication Methods used for Mealtimes:* Students with autism benefit from the use of augmentative and alternative methods for communication. Mealtimes are a highly motivating time for many students. Although many students can indicate to us what it is they want during those times through pointing and leading us to the food, it is important to encourage symbolic forms of communication. The level of communication expected will vary with the child. However, visual cues can serve as a useful tool for many students with autism. To accomplish this, try having either food logos, wrappers, actual food items, photos or picture icons of the food that the child can choose from. Have them point to, give you, or tell you, the item before consuming it. At first, you may find that some students may protest. If you are consistent during mealtimes, they will eventually learn to use a more symbolic form of communication whether it be handing a picture icon, signing or using words.

Sample Breakfast Meal Time Choice Board (use pictures for non-readers)

juice	milk	cereal
oatmeal	pancakes	help
spoon	fork	finished

-*Daily Living Skills Task Analysis:* Some of your students may have trouble with recall, sequencing and organizing. They may need some assistance in remembering the order in which things go. A visual support for routine daily living skills activities may help. For example, a set of pictures showing the steps in washing their hands or a visual task analysis for hanging up their belongings in the morning can help keep some students focused. Visual supports for routines can also help to create more independence in students.

Sample Morning Routine Support for a Student who can Read

1. Hang up backpack.
2. Hang up coat.
3. Take out lunch bag and put it in the lunch bin.
4. Take out homework folder.
5. Place homework folder in the bin.

-*Visual Cues for Supporting Positive Behavior:* As the year goes on, you will notice that several students have some challenging behaviors. Instead of constantly verbally reminding students of a classroom rule or expectation, you can visually show them what you want them to know or to do. Visual rules for behavior are helpful because the student may be more likely to look at the icon or written words, than to look at the adult. This is especially true when they are upset. Items such as pictures, iconic symbols, tape to indicate where to line up, shapes to visually cue where to sit or pictures of classroom rules, can greatly increase appropriate behaviors in some students. Linda Hodgdon's book Solving Behavior Problems in Autism is a good resource in this area.

REAL CLASSROOMS:

"I got the idea of using Velcro and magnetic tape to place the behavior (icons) all over the room from a co-worker. I could use them where I needed them. The best place to store them was under the table. I could pull out the "quiet voice" or "sit down" picture fast!"

AutismClassroom.com's Classroom Checkpoints

Classroom Setting

	1.	Data collection system is in or near each area of the setting.
	2.	Various areas of the classroom setting are present. The following areas are included and listed in the weekly schedule: -Independent work stations for each student -Sensory/sensory motor area or quiet area -Structured play/recreation-leisure area/gross motor area -Small group areas (centers, stations,1:1 or 2:1 work areas) -Large group area
	3.	Each area of the classroom has clear visual boundaries. -Good use of physical boundaries -Good use of carpets, tape, furniture
	4.	Areas of the classroom setting are labeled with pictures, picture icons or words that are obvious and easy to see from across the room.
	5.	First routine of the day is easily accessible, prepared and ready.
	6.	The setting shows that the student's belongings/desks/cubbies are clearly defined with their name/picture posted.

Keeping Students Focused

	1.	The correct number of chairs are in the room, to avoid the students need to move chairs in between activities.
	2.	Chairs and tables are the appropriate size for students.
	3.	Visual distraction levels are decreased. -Not too many visual distractions -Moving items such as banners, blinds, cords are limited or removed -Calming colors are used as background colors for bulletin boards -Distracting appliances are removed, placed out of reach or covered -Shelves are covered with fabric or curtains, if needed
	4.	Auditory distraction levels are decreased. -Loud toys reserved for specific activities -Music playing limited to non-instructional time
	5.	Low overall distractions in work areas.

Visual Strategies for Expressing and Receiving Language

	1.	Each child has their own personal individualized schedule.
	2.	Daily schedule posted, large enough, and clear.
	3.	Task schedules for independent work and table activities are present.
	4.	Daily living skills supports (hand-washing, toileting, hanging up coat/backpack) are posted by mounting photographs or picture icons with written words throughout the classroom.
	5.	Visual supports for opening/circle time are present.
	6.	Mealtime boards are available for snack, breakfast, and lunch.

	7.	Topic board for the math lesson is present.
	8.	Topic board for the reading lesson is present.
	9.	A waiting system is in place for transitions.
	10.	Visual supports and augmentative communication methods are embedded in each activity.
	11.	Covered clear containers for storing toys/activities are available. Pictures are on the outside so that students can request what is inside.
	12.	3-prompt sequence is posted on the wall as a reminder for adults.
	13.	Break times are embedded into the student's individual/personal schedule (reinforcement breaks , sensory breaks , or timed breaks, etc.)

Student Centered Planning and Individualized Planning

	1.	A data binder, folder or clipboard with data sheets, is present for each student.
	2.	Box/baggie with preferred items/reinforcers specifically chosen for that student are placed in containers or baggies and used in work areas.
	3.	1:1 work tasks are planned based on student needs.
	4.	Independent work tasks are individualized and appropriate.
	5.	Individual communication systems are available for each student, used daily.
	6.	Language is used according what the child needs and based on their individual goals.
	7.	Behavior plans are easily accessible, and all classroom team members have a copy.
	8.	Sensory needs are identified, programmed for and incorporated throughout the school day.

Organizing All of the Pieces

	1.	Data sheets are present for each IEP objective for each student.
	2.	Student goals are placed in a folder or binder that holds his or her objective for that area or activity.
	3.	Data systems are available in the area where data will be taken. Student objectives are sorted and categorized by similarities (ex. communication goals are together, fine motor objectives are together, etc.)
	4.	A Lesson Plan Binder is present with weekly lessons and tabs to separate the activities.
	5.	Lesson Plan bins are present and labeled and ready for reading, math, science, centers, sensory time, art, snack, morning activity, etc.
	6.	A written plan for classroom roles and responsibilities is posted.
	7.	Lunch and morning breaks are pre-determined and posted on the wall.
	8.	Weekly scheduled debriefing times are posted on the wall.
	9.	IEP work bin materials are stored in zippered baggies.
	10.	Organization systems are used (ex. color coding, assigned seating, routines/procedures, bins, boxes, baggies, binders, folders, etc.)
	11.	Staff are assigned to specific children/areas of class/activities and know exactly what they will be responsible for teaching and when.
	12.	Materials are stored neatly.

Student Centered Planning and Individualized Planning

Due to the nature of Special Education, student programs are individualized and based on their needs. As an educator, you will need to be certain that this occurs. Within the autism classroom, be sure to individualize the items mentioned in the paragraphs below. Student 1:1 work tasks should be individualized and specific to the child's needs as stressed on his/her IEP or IFSP. Independent work tasks that are teacher created, should take into account the child's functioning level and the skills that the child currently has in place. Each independent task should be chosen specifically for the individual child and their individual needs.

Individualization needs to occur in the area of language as well. Each student may be functioning at a different language level. This too will need to be addressed student by student. For example, if you have a student who can use words, you may have them answer with words, but if you have non-verbal students, you can have them answer using signs, pictures, written words or photos. Furthermore, if you have a student who understands pictures better than words, you will want to present information visually for that student.

As we know, reinforcers or preferred items, for each student are a necessity. If you do not have them, most often, getting the student to complete a task that you have initiated, can be difficult, to say the least. Having a box or baggie with items chosen specifically for each student, in each work area, is a useful tool for motivating students to complete work. Reinforcers or preferred items are items that the child likes, finds highly motivating, and would do some work for. They too, should be individualized and placed in that student's individual box or baggie. Some items that may work as reinforcers are sensory toys, lotion, brushes, small McDonalds's® type toys, magazines, edibles, tickles, deep pressure. For older students, provide any items the students finds motivating, not just what you think he/she should find motivating. Individualization should also be observed in behavior intervention plans. It does, however, take some time to learn to effectively write behavior plans. Chapter 10 discusses behavior plans in detail.

Organizing All of the Pieces

Organization is a key element in effectively setting up your classroom and staying on top of your beginning year or years as a teacher of students with autism. Various organizational systems such as utilizing lesson plan binders, color coding, assigned seating and established routines and procedures are needed and useful when beginning this journey. Having a good data collection system (i.e. a data recording technique or data sheet accompanies each IEP objective and is placed in the area where the data will be taken), having staff aware of all expectations related to making the day run smoothly (i.e. the roles, responsibilities, and staff breaks are clear and agreed upon) and having materials stored neatly (i.e. the student's goals are placed in a binder or folder for a specific activity, and bins/boxes or baggies binders and folders are used to effectively store and organize items) are all ways which can help bring a sense of calm and organization to any room. At times, you may find that covering shelves with plain fabric or construction paper can help to create a sense of calm as well. At the very least, it could make an unorganized shelf appear organized!

GAME PLAN:

1. Look at the weekly schedule, then create areas of the classroom that correspond to the activities listed on the schedule. Put up a sign to label each area.
2. Get each student's work bin and data binder. Get zipper baggies and a permanent marker. Write each objective that you can work on during 1:1 time on a baggie. Place the baggies in the student's bin. Repeat for all students.
3. After all the baggies are labeled, add materials to the bags that address the objective listed on the bag (For example, if the objective is to identify shapes, place 4 shapes in the bag). Start with those materials that are readily available in your classroom and do not need to be created. Repeat for all students.
4. Next, make the materials that need to be created for the work bins and add them to the bins. Repeat for all students. You will not be able to make everything in one day. Strive to get the materials made by the end of the first week of school.
5. Create and post your small groups schedule. (Use pencil. It will change.)
6. Create a reinforcer box for each student and place it in or near the work bin. Plastic food storage containers are great for this.
7. Ask a staff classroom team member to set up the independent work area with something the student can work on the first day. (Ask them to search AutismClassrom.com's "How to Set Up an Autism Class" page and click on "work task ideas.") Enhance this area at a later time.

Chapter 7

Collaborating With Others

Collaborating with others is needed for teaching students with autism. In your career you will find yourself meeting, debriefing, problem-solving and working with numerous professionals, parents and community supporters. This chapter will explore some ways in which collaboration may take place.

A Written Plan for Classroom Roles and Responsibilities

An important part of running an autism classroom is teaming. No one usually informs you while you are training for your career, that you may walk into a classroom and have two, three or four other adults there working with you on a daily basis. If you are the classroom teacher, they will be expecting you to be the instructional leader in the classroom. What a great deal of pressure that is in your first autism classroom. If you are a para-professional, the teacher will be expecting you to support the teaching endeavors. With this many people working in the class, everyone will need to build their collaboration and communication skills quick, fast and in a hurry! The most important things to remember, however, are to respect others, empower others, motivate others, write down expectations, verbally discuss the written expectations and give each person in the room a copy of the written expectations.

A written plan for classroom roles and responsibilities will be helpful in creating an organized and effective classroom staff team. Having everyone on the "same page" and aware of their individual responsibilities helps each person function efficiently as part of that team. It is usually a good idea to have a written plan that designates the major responsibilities that each staff member assumes, posted up somewhere in the room. The plan should include the areas of the classroom that each staff member is responsible for during the instructional parts of the day, as well as any items the team member will do before and after school. For example, tasks such as running the art lesson, preparing the snack activity, supporting the language lesson, and preparing the daily calendar for the next day, may be the types of responsibilities noted.

In order to find out what the roles and responsibilities will be for each team member, take a look at your weekly schedule and see what tasks need to be done in order to make each activity run efficiently. After you have established the activities that will take place during the day, _and_ what needs to be done to prepare and implement them, then sit down with the team members to plan. As a team, have each person establish their morning break (if applicable) and their lunch break time. (Try your best to schedule activities which can be handled by a smaller amount of staff members during all the lunch break times. For example, recess, sensory time, structured play may be activities the students enjoy and stay focused on and can be handled by a smaller number of staff members.) Once all staff members, **_including you_**, have established lunch break times, it will be easier to finish the roles and responsibilities chart. There will be some items where there is no doubt that the classroom teacher will need to take the lead for that role or responsibility. However, there will be several activities and tasks that can be shared or can be completed by any person on the team. Start with the items the classroom teacher definitely has to conduct or address. After those are listed, then talk with the team about activities they have a skill at doing or an interest in doing. For example, if you have a person who is very skilled at art, they could possibly be in charge of creating ideas and scenery for the bulletin boards or running the art lesson for the classroom. Another example could be if you have a person who loves to sing, they could possibly run the opening morning circle part of the day, while including lots of music.

At times, you will notice that some of the responsibilities overlap and can be done by more than one person. When that occurs, that is fine. At least one person is assigned to that task, even if others choose to help. But remember, as the classroom teacher, that person should be willing and ready to do everything that is on that list if the need arises! That includes toilet training when necessary.

Classrooms serving students with autism require a great deal of teamwork; a plan in which responsibilities are clarified will positively contribute to the productivity of the team.

REAL CLASSROOMS:

"In our classroom the para-professionals run the fine motor activity and the play lesson. We already know the theme for the week, the teacher provides us with a general outline for how she wants the lessons to be conducted with a warm-up, a specific objective and a closure activity to review the concepts. We write a quick, short lesson plan. She just asks that we provide her with the plan the Thursday before the lessons are going to be taught."

Debriefing

Debriefing is another aspect of collaborating with others. It will be very important to meet with your team members on a regular basis to debrief and review the instructional strategies that you are using in the classroom. Sometimes team members will have questions for one another that they cannot ask and get a good answer to when the students are present. When the students are there, all of the adult's time and energy is dedicated to the students. Creating a specific time to meet, answer questions or create new plans is a great idea. It gives you a time to sit and talk without being rushed. Determining a day and time and hanging a reminder on the wall will help everyone on the team to remember.

Collaborating with Professionals

In the past, related service providers would take the student out of the classroom to provide therapy. This is typically referred to as a "pull–out" model. However, the current model in which many school systems are embracing is the trans-disciplinary model. In the trans-disciplinary model, some services from providers are conducted in the setting in which the child will need the skills. Most often this setting is the student's classroom. Also, in this model, services are looked at as a shared responsibility of the student's team (Downing & Bailey 1990). This means that teachers and related service providers will need to work on some of the goals and objectives as a team. With the guidance and techniques from the related service provider, each member of the student's classroom team is responsible for implementing and working with that student on reaching that goal or objective. For this to occur, interpersonal skills and the ability to interact with different personalities is a must. Sometimes worlds will collide and everyone will not always see on the "same page." As a new educator, or an educator new to an autism classroom, it might be helpful to dust off that old college interpersonal communications book or explore current literature on collaboration skills and methods.

ReAL CLASSROOMS:

"I learned so much from the OT and Speech specialist my first year. That shaped the way I teach. My students are better off because of the learning that went on between me and the specialists."

Talking with Parents

Communication with parents is also essential in a classroom the serves students with autism. It is important for teachers to communicate with parents so that parents are aware of what is happening in their child's life. Many parents may need you to be the connection to what happened that day at school, if they have a child who cannot verbally tell them. To do this, you may find it effective to keep a notebook or journal that is sent from school to home each day. Using this method, both the teacher and the parents can write what happened in their environment and send it to the other environment. Please keep in mind that some parent's lives are so hectic, that they may not be able to write back every day. However, these same parents are able to read what happened, so it will be important for you to continue to write and possibly create a system for the parents for them to let you know they read the message. (Perhaps they could fold the page down or check the page to let you know they read the entry.) Another method could be to use pictures and have students check, mark or circle, the picture that represents what activity they participated in that day.

Ways to Respect, Empower and Motivate Each Other...

Respect	Empower	Motivate
1. Truly understand that you need each other to make the classroom work.	1. Listen to others.	1. Discuss problem situations as a team. Do not single out any one team member. If you make a set of guidelines they are for everyone, review them with everyone. Present them to everyone with a similar format "Here is what is happening. Here is what we will try to do in the future."
2. Say please and thank-you.	2. Create a roles and responsibilities chart.	2. Bringing in food to say thanks always works!!
3. Don't expect anyone to do a task you would not do or do not do yourself.	3. Have team members lead specific lessons with direction from the classroom teacher regarding the elements to include in the lesson.	3. Praise specific things a team member has done well. Encourage them to keep up the good work.
4. Prepare and inform your team ahead a time of plans or changes in plans for the school day.	4. Ask a team member to become the expert or take the lead in a certain area of classroom programming (ex. communication, making visual supports for each activity, making work tasks, teaching the team about sensory information and ideas, etc.	4. Say please and thank-you.
5. Listen and consider others ideas. Even if you do not go with the idea, at least consider the pros and cons of the idea.	5. Use the terms "we," "let's," "team members," and "our." Try to reduce "I" and "my."	5. Plan specific tasks or items of your choosing, with your team members on a regular basis. Gather input from everyone.

SAMPLE
Classroom Roles and Responsibilities

Staff:___Jan_____	Staff :___Kevin_____	Staff:__Mary__
Prepare Work Bins Play	Prepare Fine Motor Bin	Prepare Structured
Prepare Reading Bin	Prepare Calendar and	Lesson
Grooming Activity	Daily Schedule	Prepare Art Bin
CBI Lessons	Make Student Schedules	Attendance
Wipe tables	Stack Chairs	Lunch Count
Math Snacks	Independent Work Area	Get needed PCS
Prepare Social Skills box		Update Sensory
Lesson		

LUNCH BREAKS:

Time	Staff
11:00 -11:30	Jan
11:30 - 12:00	Kevin
12:00 - 12:30	Mary

MORNING BREAKS:

Time	Staff
----	----
10:30	Kevin
10:45	Mary

S.Linton 11/01

SAMPLE #2
Classroom Roles and Responsibilities

Jan (11:00 - 11:30 lunch)
Prepare work bins with work materials and preferred items boxes for each student.
Prepare reading lesson and gather materials for the lesson.
Prepare math lesson and gather materials for the lesson.
Read student notebooks as they enter.
Conduct morning toileting routine.
Conduct tooth brushing and hand washing activity after lunch.
Run Center 1.
Plan field trips.
Wipe tables after school.
Prepare Social Skills lessons for the students. Conduct the Social Skills lesson.
Bus duty in the PM.
Take data on student's objectives.
Follow student's toileting protocols.
Read and implement each student's behavior plan each day.
Attend weekly debriefing meetings.

Kevin (11:30 - 12:00 lunch)
Prepare Morning Work bin each afternoon, for the next day.
Prepare the calendar and daily schedule each afternoon, for the next day.
Prepare student schedules for the next day.
Bus duty in the AM and PM.
Stack chairs after school.
Run Center 2.
Run the independent work lesson.
Plan and conduct the structured play activities.
Take data on student's objectives.
Follow student's toileting protocols.
Read and implement each student's behavior plan each day.
Attend weekly debriefing meetings.

Mary (12:00 - 12:30 lunch)
Guide students to hang up backpacks and belongings as they arrive.
Bus duty in the PM.
Update and maintain the sensory box.
Gather and submit attendance and lunch count.
Run Center 3.
Prepare art lessons materials.
Decorate the bulletin boards, as needed.
Gather needed picture symbols, photos and props for lessons for the week.
Follow student's toileting protocols.
Read and implement each student's behavior plan each day.
Attend weekly debriefing meetings.

Classroom Roles and Responsibilities

Staff _____   Staff _____   Staff _____

LUNCH BREAKS:

Time   **Staff**

___to___   _____
___to___   _____
___to___   _____

MORNING BREAKS:

Time   **Staff**

_____   _____
_____   _____
_____   _____

S.Linton11/01

GAME PLAN:

1. Establish break and lunch break times.

2. Create a roles and responsibility chart for your classroom team.

3. Set up a debriefing time.

4. Create a notebook or journal to communicate back and forth to the parents.

5. Schedule in a specific time to write in the parent notebooks each day during a 15-minute activity which other members of your team are conducting. (For example, story time at the end of the day, music time at the end of the day, or computer time may be good times for this.)

Chapter 8

Language Based Techniques/AAC Embedded in Activities

Language Based Techniques or Augmentative and Alternative Communication (AAC) strategies must be embedded in activities throughout the student's day. AAC strategies are methods which help to augment or help the student's communication. The goal is to make sure that language is being received and expressed by students in each activity. Remember, it is equally important that the adults make sure the students understand what is being communicated, as well as having the students communicate. These materials will take some time to make, but they will be well worth it.

Examples of Activities Where Visual Supports are Needed...

*Toileting	*Transition Areas	*Snack	*Cooking Lesson
*Dressing	*Sensory Area	*Art	*Work Time
*Hand-Washing	*Play Time	*Music	*Opening/Circle
*Group Lessons	*Story		*Anywhere you have to communicate

This chapter could be an entire book by itself, so I am only going to highlight some ways in which you can include AAC in your classroom. In her book, Meaningful Exchanges for People with Autism, Joanne Cafiero describes several AAC strategies for use in classrooms. This highly recommended book, provides great insight into the various strategies. Cafiero mentions Natural Aided Language (NAL), Sign Language, Visual Symbols, and AAC Devices (no tech, low-tech, and high-tech) in detail.

AAC Strategies
(The information in this insert is from Meaningful Exchanges for People with Autism, Cafiero, 2005)

Natural Aided Language- A model of reciprocal give and take communication which utilizes the "mother tongue" method of learning language. It implies that both communication partners are giving and receiving
language input. Symbols are often used to help language output and input.
Sign Language- An unaided AAC method in which manual signs are used as a form of communication. For some students, the visual input of the sign is more reinforcing than the verbal words alone and may help them to understand the task. Some students will be able to physically produce the signs and others may only be able to make approximations.
Visual Symbols- Visual symbols can take many forms from object representation, to photographs, to line drawings, to written words. In either case, they provide a concrete image to which the student can refer when communicating. Visual symbols play an important part in a classroom for students with autism. They are your most needed tool.
No-Tech Devices- AAC strategies or tools which have no batteries, electronic components or voice output.
Low-Tech Devices- Simple voice output devices that are capable of playing back a few seconds to eight minutes of recorded speech.
High Tech Devices- Complex voice output devices that are capable of playing back eight minutes or more of recorded or digitized speech. These devices also have changeable grids and overlays for individualized programming.

AAC supports are such a big part of teaching students with autism since we know that many students with autism are visual learners. Visual supports help them to understand the language used by the adult. Many times the adult will say something, but it will take a few seconds for that message to register with the student. By that time, the adult is onto the second part of the message and the student is still trying to figure out the first part. By using visual supports, the message can still be there even after the adult has said it, thus giving the child time to register the message.

Books and Websites with of Visual Supports:

Visual Strategies for Improving Communication (Linda Hodgdon)
Solving Behavior Problems in Autism   (Linda Hodgdon)
Meaningful Exchanges for People with Autism (Joanne Cafiero)
A Picture's Worth (Andrew Bondy & Lori Frost)
Task Galore: Making Groups Meaningful (Fennell, Hearsey & Eckenrode)

www.uscvisualstrategies.com
www.mayerjohnson.com
www.specialed.us/autism/assist/asst10.htm

Language Lessons

When it comes time to plan your actual lessons you will need to be creative in order to gain the attention and keep the attention of some of your students.   Increasing receptive language in the students can happen throughout your group lessons. One of the most effective ways to make this happen is to use real objects and hands on materials as much as possible. This would mean that if you were presenting a lesson about going on a vacation, for example, in addition to talking about the items to be packed in a suitcase or having pictures of the items one might pack, you would bring in an actual suitcase and the real items for the students to pack inside. This type of hands on lesson will help build language connections with the students and make the lesson more interesting.

Some Other Pointers For Conducting Lessons Would Be To:

- Have your materials ready in a box or bin before the lesson begins.
- Only keep on the table the items you are discussing at the present time. Do not clutter the table with extra things.
- Use hands on activities as much as possible.
- Keep your materials for the lesson behind you or they may end up on the floor.
- Use a topic board to show the students what the lesson will be about.
- Use a topic board to review the lesson at the end. Always close out the lesson with a quick (could be only 30 seconds) review of what was discussed.
- Remember to alternate sides when presenting to each student. Don't feel the need to always work from the student on the left side to the student on the right side.
- Remember to transition the students. Clearly let them know the lesson is finished by telling them or showing them a sign. Also, always direct them to the next activity.

GAME PLAN:

1. Think about the language that you may use in each activity.

2. Practice using the software in your school which makes picture icons.

3. Laminate about 7 pieces of construction paper or use cut foam board to use as topic boards. For the laminated ones, you will be able to tape on any picture icons you need for the activity. This method will work until you can make all of the different boards you may need.

4. Request batteries from the school for any low-tech or high-tech communication devices you have in your class.

5. Ask a team member to ask a co-worker how to program the low-tech or high-tech communication device. Have them show everyone at your next debriefing meeting.

6. This next step takes time and you may have to give it a few weeks: Create a topic board or visual communication method for breakfast time, lunch, snack, opening, each center area, music, art, reading lesson, math lesson, sensory tine, play time, the bathroom area, hanging coats and book bags and any other area you think you may need.

Chapter 9

Making Smooth Transitions

Smooth transitions are created when educators provide consistent routines and procedures. Establishing a "waiting area" within the classroom can provide students with an organized and predictable place to sit or stand during some of the class's daily transitions. Examples of methods used in creating waiting areas include, but are not limited to, chairs, shapes taped to the floor, cut-out paper foot prints, and masking tape. Regardless of the method used, the concept is the same: to provide a visual cue to the students of where they are to wait. In addition to a waiting area, some educators choose to provide the students with a card which says "wait" to help the child visually see that they are waiting.

There are some times when a waiting area just is not enough. The following information is provided for those students who present difficulties with making transitions. If this in an issue for a student in your class, before the next activity begins, try creating a box or bag with reinforcers or toys that the student likes. This box or bag should be visible to him or her before he or she comes to that area to work. This may motivate him or her transition to the area. If not, try the suggestions on the next page.

REAL CLASSROOMS:

"We used our class schedule that was on the chalkboard to make transitions. When the lesson was over we'd have the kids look at the schedule to see what was next."

Easing Difficult Transitions

1. Have something the student really likes at the place where the student has to transition to each time.

2. Let the student carry something or "help" you to the next activity (schedule cards, picture icons, or the materials for the lesson may work well) and establish what this item will be before the moment arrives.

3. Let the student hold something when they are sitting at the activity. (Your first goal is to have the student join the group, you can work on having the student participate later.)

4. Give the student a 1-2 minute warning **every time any activity is almost finished** and a visual cue (ex. picture icon which states "one minute.")

5. Physically guide (using the least amount of physical contact necessary), the student to the next activity, without giving him or her the opportunity to stray from the group, or go to the wrong place. Holding a hand works for most students.

6. Hold the student's hand before you make the request for them to transition so that you will decrease their opportunity to run to the wrong area.

7. Use a count-down routine or a visual count-down to show the students that an activity is coming to an end. Take each icon or object off one at a time at various times to prepare them for the end of an activity.

8. Have a topic board in each activity area for the student to communicate his wants and needs. The topic board should also include "finished" and "clean-up," so that the student is aware that a transition is about to occur.

The following information was given to me by a mentor my first year of teaching. It is very useful advice for teaching students with autism:

Transitions

When making transitions always use simple concrete language (very few words).

Example: "Opening is finished. (Pause.) Time for Reading."

GAME PLAN:

1. Post the transitions sign in the room to remind adults to tell the students about a transition.

2. Create a waiting area or a waiting system before the first day. Share your vision of this system with your team before the students arrive. Choose one adult to always stand or sit in close proximity to the waiting area until the transition is complete. Otherwise, some students might continuously get up and walk away.

3. Create a transition box or bin with small toys or books that are easy to clean up.

Chapter 10

Functional Behavior Assessments and Behavior Intervention Plans

The information you will learn in this chapter is not a set of skills that one develops in one day. This information may take you some time to read and re-read several times to fully get the impact. It will take even longer to implement some of the strategies, as you will only know from first hand experience with your students, exactly which section of this chapter will work for your situation. With that said, many students with autism present some behavior or set of behaviors which can be challenging. When these behaviors are presented, quite often, typical solutions to intervene which may work for a typical child, are often unsuccessful for some children with autism. Educators and parents must educate themselves about the disability of autism and the information about Functional Behavior Assessment and their link to creating a solid Behavior Intervention Plan. When you are first starting out, dealing with difficult behaviors is often a huge concern for new teachers, paraprofessionals and administrators working with students with autism. Also, more often than not, people believe they must get the behavior under "control" or that they must devise a consequence for the behavior, without really looking at all of the things they can do ahead of time to eliminate the behavior in the first place. In order to effectively reduce some behaviors, you have to work on preventative measures. These preventative measures are now more commonly called Positive Behavior Supports or PBS (www.PBIS.org). First and foremost, in your class you will need to have a good classroom set up, have consistent routines, and use visual supports to show students the expectations. The following table includes a long list of _some_ preventative measures to use before a behavior occurs or before you develop a reaction plan to any behavior.

Positive Behavior Supports: Ask yourself, are these items in place? ...

Class structure- needs to be in place for real, not just in theory
Consistent routines for all activities throughout the day
Pre-made and prepared activities with all materials ready
Pre-assigned roles and responsibilities throughout the day for staff members
Pre-determined and labeled areas for activities
Limited auditory and visual distractions such as music and hanging items
Proximity control (staying close by)
Clear expectations expressed by using icons or visual signs or written words
Individual student schedules to allow for independence and ownership
A daily class schedule which promotes movement throughout the day
Tone of voice -try whispering to calm the atmosphere or use a neutral voice tone
Few/limited words to express what you want the student to do
Provide visual cues and gestures/models along with or instead of verbal language
Offer a less favored activity first, then a highly preferred activity
Relocate the activity or people if a problem behavior keeps happening in the same area or with the same person
Provide highly motivating activities to help the student through a difficult activity
Removal of problem items before the student enters the room (ex. Soda cans, water bottles)
Change to positive body language- try not to stand over the student or present negative body language (ex. Folded arms, frustrated facial expressions)
Awareness of sensory issues in the child's environment and a respect for the student that the sensory input may be causing a problem or may be painful
Decrease of difficult tasks by decreasing in numbers, time, or requirements
Provision of a slight physical prompt, if needed, to make the task easier
Access to highly preferred items for positive behavior
Use of visuals to show the child what reward they will get for positive behavior
Make other school members and the principal aware of your plan

If you have these items in place you will probably have prevented many behaviors from becoming an issue. However, you will still have some behaviors in the classroom which are undesirable. At that point, it is time to look a tool called a Functional Behavior Assessment. A Functional Behavior Assessment (FBA) is a process in which you observe the individual and take data in order to find out **why** the person is engaging in the behavior. You then develop a plan based on why the student is engaging in the behavior (www.PBIS.org). Since it is thought that all behavior is communicative and all behavior is purposeful, the theory behind FBA is that the behavior serves a function or a purpose for that person. By conducting a Functional Behavior Assessment, you try to identify the function that the behavior serves (ex. why is the person doing this behavior?) In order to come up with a Behavior Intervention Plan that works for that particular student, and that particular behavior, you must first correctly identify the function.

Functional Behavioral Assessments take time to complete because you need to observe the individual and ask many questions to find out if there are any patterns in the student's behavior. For example, "Do they engage in the behavior with one person, but not another?" or "Does the behavior only happen in the morning?" are both some of the types of questions you will want to know the answers to when conducting an FBA. These observations, when written down and data is collected about them, can sometimes help to identify a pattern of behavior. This, in turn, may offer an idea of the function or purpose that behavior serves for that student. When conducting an FBA several assessment tools may be used. Data collection sheets of various styles, direct observation, interviews, and questioning of the adults who work closely with the student, are a few of the assessment tools that may be useful to a team trying to find answers.

First   Then

FBA   BIP

When beginning your search to identify the function of the behavior, you must first start by specifically identifying the **target behavior** in question. It is not enough to say the student is "aggressive" or has "outbursts." These descriptors are too vague. When identifying the target behavior, you will need to be extremely specific.

Examples of **target behavior** descriptions which are vague and *not useful*

- aggressive
- has outbursts
- runs away all the time
- screams at adults
- grabs food all the time
- off task

Examples of **target behavior** descriptions which are *very specific and useful:*

- hits other students and adults when asked to do work tasks
- screams, cries, kicks and throws items when upset
- leaves the group activity, without adult permission several times a day
- uses a loud voice to communicate with adults when he is corrected
- takes food from others plates during lunch, snack and at home
- plays with fingers or pencil during work time

Once you have specifically identified the target behavior(s), you can begin to start observing and keeping data for that behavior. If you have a student with many behaviors, it is helpful to only work on a few behaviors at a time (maybe 1 or 2) in order to be truly effective. This means, that some behaviors will be ignored while you are working on the targeted behaviors. To observe and keep good data, you will need to determine what type of data sheet to use. Having good data will allow you to report objectively about the behavior. The information will be in black and white and leave no room for subjective opinions about what is occurring with the student and the behavior. If your data is clear, it will be easier to explain to a parent or administrator what is occurring in the classroom with the student. Using the examples of specific target behaviors from the previous page, below are some identified options (options are italicized) for collecting data on that behavior:

Recording Inappropriate Behaviors

hits other students and adults when asked to do work tasks *~~this behavior may require some type of data collection which focuses on frequency. You will want to record how many times a day this behavior occurs. It would also be helpful for you to include the time and activity each hit occurs. If you have an individual that hits "all day" you will want to record each and every hit.*

screams, cries, kicks and throws items when upset *~~this behavior may require some type of data collection which focuses on intensity or duration. You may want to record how long the screaming, crying, kicking, throwing episodes last or you may want to record how intense they are. For example, sometimes the person may cry, but other times, he/she may cry, kick and throw items. The activity and time the behavior happens is also important to record.*

leaves the group activity, without adult permission several times a day *~~this behavior may require some type of data collection which focuses on frequency. You will want to record how many times this behavior occurs during each activity. Maybe use a data chart which has the daily schedule and requires the adults to place tally marks each time the child leaves that activity. If you have an individual that leaves the group activity several times a day, you will want to record each and every time.*

uses a loud voice to communicate with adults when he is corrected *~~this behavior may require some type of data collection which focuses on finding out why he is "yelling." An ABC data chart may be handy for this. With an ABC data chart you can identify the Antecedent, Behavior and Consequence (ABC) for the behavior. With an ABC data chart you would record what happened right before the behavior (ex. what did the teacher say when correcting his work), then you record the behavior, next, you record the consequence. The consequence is simply whatever happens after the child engages in the behavior (ex. does the adult leave him alone, does the adult say something back, or does the adult ignore the yelling.)*

takes food from others plates during lunch, snack and at home *~~this behavior may require some type of data collection which focuses on frequency. You will want to record how many attempts the person has at taking food as well as actual successes with taking food. It may be helpful to collect data on what type of food the child is trying to take and what is already on his/her plate. In addition, you may want to record the ABC's of this behavior, because you will want to know what the reaction of the adult is after the child takes the food. This will be important in determining the function of the behavior.*

plays with fingers or pencil during work time *~~this behavior may require some type of data collection which focuses on duration or intervals. You will want to record how many reminders the adult needs to provide the child before he completes or focuses on the work or how long the child waits from the time the direction is given until he/she starts working.*

After you have identified the target behavior, and collected some data, it is now time to explore possible functions for behaviors. Typically, you will hear people say there are 4 major functions for behaviors. Others will say there are 5 or 6 functions. I am going to explore the four typical functions that are usually addressed. These four functions are listed below (Bruce, Gurdin & Savage, 2006).

- Escape / Avoidance
- Gaining Attention
- Gaining a Tangible Item
- Sensory Input Derived from the Behavior

How To Tell What the Function Could Be...

Some possible indicators of **escape/avoidance** reinforcement are:
- The individual engages in the behavior when a task is presented
- The individual engages in the behavior when a new activity begins
- The individual engages in the behavior when a stimuli *they* view/perceive as aversive is presented
- The behavior ends when the student is allowed to leave the activity

Some possible indicators of **attention gained** reinforcement are:
- Attention (words, eye contact, body language) reliably/usually follows the behavior
- The individual looks at or approaches a caregiver before engaging in the behavior
- The individual smiles just before engaging in the behavior

Some possible indicators of **access to a tangible item** reinforcement are:
- The individual's behavior ends when given the item or activity
- The individual asks for/requests the item
- The individual's behaviors occur after it is clear that they cannot have the item they want
- The individual's behavior occurs when the item is not presented fast enough

Some possible indicators of **sensory** reinforcement are:
- The individual would engage in the behavior even when other people are not present
- The individual appears to be engaging in the behavior because they need sensory input (ex. Pushing up against others, mouthing objects, squeezing others, banging tables, hands in ears, rolling on the floor, running around the room, getting up out of seat, etc.)
- The individual appears to be enjoying the behavior, not aware of others around them, not being presented with a work activity, and not attempting to gain access to something

After you have identified the function or at least have a good idea of what you think the function of the behavior may be, then it will then be time to come up with some solutions to addressing the target behavior. Depending on the function of the behavior, your response will be different. For example, if the student's behavior is maintained by gaining attention for the behavior, you and your team will have to stop providing attention for that inappropriate behavior. Another example might be if a student is using a behavior because he wants to escape a task, you and your team may have to figure out a way to make the task easier and provide him with a break (escape) before he takes it upon himself to take the break. You can always add on more time or work gradually. For sensory maintained behaviors, talk with the Occupational Therapist to see if they have some ideas for you. If not, you can provide the input the child needs on a regular basis throughout the day. If a student's function is determined to be their access to a tangible item that they want, you and your team can work with the student to learn to request the item in an appropriate manner opposite from the target behavior. Each of these suggestions is only one of many possible solutions for a Behavior Intervention Plan. Please know that this is only a small portion of what there is to know regarding interventions. With any Behavior Intervention Plan, it will be important to inform other staff members in the school about the techniques you will be using, so that they are not inadvertently hurting the plan. Also, Positive Behavior Supports, like those listed on page 65 will be your best defense for keeping inappropriate behaviors out of your classroom.

A Few Intervention Ideas

If the Function is …	Try one of these options…
Escape or Avoid a Situation	• Put in place Positive Behavior Supports • Provide a scheduled "escape" before the student engages in the behavior • Decrease the difficulty of the activity, then gradually increase the difficulty • Teach the student to request a break appropriately • Do not stop the activity because of the behavior
Attention from Others	• Put in place Positive Behavior Supports • Do not provide attention for inappropriate behavior (no eye contact, no verbal comments, neutral body language) • Assist the student into a safe situation without verbal comments • Provide an over abundance of attention on a scheduled basis for appropriate behavior and reward for appropriate behavior
Gain Access to a Tangible Item	• Put in place Positive Behavior Supports • Teach an appropriate way to ask for the item or activity • Teach the student to "wait" using a wait card, timer, or first-then board • Use visual supports to show the student when he or she will get the item or activity or to show the item is no longer available
Sensory Input Gained from Behavior	• Put in place Positive Behavior Supports • Talk with an Occupational Therapist • Provide appropriate sensory input before the student needs it or provide it on a regular basis • Provide an alternate behavior that may give the student the same type of sensory input

SAMPLE
Behavior Intervention Plan "Planner"

Target Behavior: Leaving the group during a group activity.

Possible Function: **Escape behavior to avoid demands** and avoid teacher instructions.

Strategies to Increase Appropriate Behaviors:
-visual personal schedule
-mini-task schedule for each activity
-rearrange tables and chairs
- place a staff member behind the student
- place toys on the table as an incentive to stay seated. Fade them later.
-reinforcement schedule with a reward for the student for remaining seated for X number of seconds or minutes

Strategies to Decrease Inappropriate Behaviors:
-3 prompt sequence to bring them back to the table
-eliminate or limit verbal comments for inappropriate behavior

Skills to be Taught:
-use of personal schedule
-functional communication training to request a break or an activity
-how to use the mini-task schedule

Supports Needed:
Staff, visual supports for schedules, incentive box or toys, reinforcement schedule and preferred items

SAMPLE
Behavior Intervention Plan "Planner"

Target Behavior: Refusing to sit on the toilet independently.

Possible Function: **Sensory**. Not aware of the need to go.

Strategies to Increase Appropriate Behaviors:
-visual task analysis in the bathroom area
-use pants with elastic waistband instead of zippers
-visual timer to time student's time on the toilet
-"Good Job" sign for success
-preferred items box in bathroom to keep the student in the bathroom area
-Social Story (made famous by Carol Gray) about bathroom expectations or the story can be used to ease the student's fears about the bathroom area

Strategies to Decrease Inappropriate Behaviors:
-planned ignoring of protests to sitting on the toilet
-3 prompt sequence to help the student follow through
-keep the student distracted with preferred activities while they are waiting for the timer to go off
-work on one skill at a time—first sitting on the toilet for a period of time

Skills to be Taught:
-waiting
-sequencing

Supports Needed: timer, sign, Social Story, pictures related to toileting, plastic box, preferred items for the student, time

SAMPLE
Behavior Intervention Plan "Planner"

Target Behavior: Dropping to the Floor (no aggressive behaviors included) for attention.

Possible Function: **Attention** from the adult.

Strategies to Increase Appropriate Behaviors:
-visual personal schedule
-mini-task schedule for each activity
-place toys on the table as an incentive
-give the child something to carry
-give them a job to do between activities to keep focused
- sing on the way to the next activity
-praise the students who walk to the activity without dropping

Strategies to Decrease Inappropriate Behaviors:
-do not call the child's name after he or she has dropped
-do not talk to the child after he or she has dropped
-hold the child's hand and wait for him or her to get up (this has taken up to 20 minutes for some people. However, overall, it only took about a week or more to change the behavior, so plan ahead)
-do not make eye contact with the child during the intervention
-do not talk to others about the child's behavior while you are working with the child
-keep a calm, neutral body tone and try not to talk
-when the child stands up, walk them to the area in which they are supposed to be and proceed with the lesson. Try not to mention the inappropriate behavior they just displayed.

Skills to be Taught:
-picture recognition
-use of schedule

Supports Needed: Staff, visual supports for schedules, incentive box or toys, and preferred items

Blank form. Please Reprint as you wish.

Behavior Intervention Plan "Planner"

Target Behavior:

Possible Function:

Strategies to Increase Appropriate Behaviors:

Strategies to Decrease Inappropriate Behaviors:

Skills to be Taught:

Supports Needed:

3- Prompt Sequence

The 3-prompt sequence I learned from a mentor. It is a strategy to use when you want a student to follow through on a request. The more consistent that staff members are with having students follow through, the more consistent students will become in following adult directions. The 3 prompt sequence helps students increase appropriate behaviors and helps staff members in two ways:

1. It helps students who have receptive language difficulties and may not understand what is being asked of them.
2. It helps students who may understand the direction, but just may be non-compliant, to follow through the with task (with assistance from the adult).

The 3-prompt sequence is a useful tool for many everyday instructions given to your students. However, if a student has a specific behavior plan for specific targeted behaviors, please identify, as a team, when it would NOT be beneficial to use the 3-prompt sequence (ex. If a child required a planned ignoring strategy for specific behavior, do not use 3-prompt sequence for that specific behavior.)

Use 3- prompt sequence whenever you want a student to do something (ex. Get coat on, wash hands, share toys, follow instructions.) Here are the prompts:

3-Prompt Sequence

Prompt 1-VERBALLY tell the student what you want him or her to do.

Prompt 2-GESTURE or MODEL to the student what to do and repeat the request.

Prompt 3-HELP the student to complete the request.

GAME PLAN:

1. Brace yourself because you are about to see some things you never thought you would see when you envisioned your teaching career.

2. Be understanding. Do not take the student's behavior challenges personally. Do not over react to ANYTHING. Remain professional and calm when trying to figure out an intervention for a challenging behavior.

3. Teach yourself how to remain calm when the world around you seems to be falling apart.

4. Read this chapter over again 2 more times.

5. Read each student's file to see if there are any interventions that are already proven to work for him or her.

6. Concentrate heavily on setting up your room to avoid behavior challenges and use Positive Behavior Supports to increase appropriate behavior. Do this even when the behavior seems to be completely out of your area of expertise. Focus on what you can do to promote the behavior you want from the student.

7. Remember that your reaction to the behavior will either keep the behavior occurring or cause the behavior to eventually stop. So if the behavior continues, change your reaction.

Chapter 11

Sensory Differences

I want to start this chapter by stating, I am not an expert in the field of sensory issues. However, I think there are a few items you will want to know before stepping into an autism classroom for the first time. Individuals with autism sometimes experience sensory input differently than others. When this occurs, these differences affect the student's response to the world around them, their behavior, the way in which they learn and the manner in which they relate to others (Kranowitz, 1998). When people think of the senses, we typically think of five senses; sight, smell, taste, touch and hearing. When discussing sensory issues with students with autism, we must also include two other senses which are the vestibular sense and the proprioceptive sense. The vestibular sense allows your body to understand where and how it is moving in space; It is responsible for a person's balance and movement from the neck, eyes and body (Kranowitz, 1998). The proprioceptive system refers to the sense in our body which tells us about body awareness and body position perceived through our muscles, joints, ligaments, tendons and connective tissue (Kranowitz, 1998).

When interacting with your students, you may notice that some of your students may seem to over react or under react to some sensory input in one of these seven areas. Both of which could possibly affect the behavior of the student. It will be important for you to know about the sensory differences in each of your students and to respect their differences, while also trying to make your classroom a place in which the students can thrive and learn. Sometimes sensory issues can make it difficult for a student to concentrate or to tolerate a particular smell, sound or sight. The behavior they may use to avoid that smell, sound or sight, may be misconstrued by the adult as defiance, when in fact, there may be a sensory issue they are trying to avoid. It is a good idea to talk with the Occupational Therapist in your school building to get professional advice regarding sensory issues. They are the experts in this area. They can give you strategies to help the student to calm, organize and focus themselves throughout the school day. My goal is just to provide you with some information to get your school year started. Please use this information only as a beginning step to learning more about sensory differences in autism. As you learn more by reading and talking with the Occupational Therapist, you will be better equipped to develop and provide interventions to assist your students.

Below, there is a chart highlighting some of signs that may indicate to you that a student is experiencing sensory input differently. The information is only a portion of indicators that could be present. Each section lists the indicators you might see if the student is either over-responsive or under-responsive in that particular sensory input. In the chart, over-responsive reactions and under-responsive reactions are not separated.

The information in this table was obtained from the book <u>The Out of Sync Child</u> by Carol Stock Kranowitz (1998). Her book provides detailed information, strategies and activities for addressing each area.

Sensory Area	Possible Indicators
Touch	• Fearful, anxious or aggressive when touched lightly or unexpectedly • Becomes afraid when touched from behind or by someone or something they are not able to see • Avoids or dislikes playing in sand, mud, water, glue, foam, etc. • Will not wear clothes with certain textures • Picky eater • Seeks out touch, appears to need to touch everything and everyone • Is not aware of being touched or bumped • Puts objects in mouth often
Vision	• Easily distracted by visual stimuli in the room (ex. Movement, decoration, toys, doorways) • Does not make or makes limited eye contact • Notices details or patterns and not the larger picture • Difficulty finding differences in pictures, words, symbols or objects
Hearing	• Distracted by sounds that do not typically affect others (ex. Humming of lights or refrigerators, fans or clocks) • Startled by loud or unexpected sounds • Might put hands over ears • Does not answer when name is called • Listens to excessively loud music or TV
Smell	• Unusual response to smells which don't bother others • May not eat certain foods due to smell • Irritated by strong scents • Difficulty discriminating unpleasant odors • Fails to pay attention to unpleasant odors
Taste	• Picky eater • Prefers to eat hot or cold foods • Puts objects in mouth often • Drools a lot
Proprioceptive	• Likes jumping and crashing activities • Enjoys being wrapped tight in weighted blankets • May hit, bump or push others often • Uses too little or too much force with objects • Difficulty catching self if falling
Vestibular	• Avoids moving playground equipment • Afraid of having feet leave the ground • Does not like rapid or rotating movement • Constantly moving • Could spin for hours and does not appear dizzy • Seeks out fast, spinning and intense movement

What is a Sensory Diet?...

A sensory diet is a planned and scheduled activity program that an Occupational Therapist develops to help a person become more self-regulated; it consists of multi-sensory experiences that a person seeks each day to satisfy their sensory appetite (Kranowitz, 1998). The goal of a sensory diet is to provide the sensory input the student craves on a regular and planned basis to help keep the student functioning at his or her best. The staff in the classroom would provide the sensory experiences that the student needs throughout the day in various activities. The sensory diet is individualized and based on the needs and preferences of that particular student.

GAME PLAN:

1. Read the student's file to see if he or she has any unique sensory needs.

2. Talk to the Occupational Therapist about providing you with information for specific students.

3. Start a list during the first 2 weeks of school to note what types of sensory experiences the student likes and dislikes. Contact the student's parents for more information about the student's likes and dislikes.

Chapter 12

Resources

I hope the information in this book has been helpful to you in your quest to set up or enhance your autism classroom. This information was meant to be merely a starting point for you. I encourage you to continue your quest for a great classroom through reading, observing other good teachers and by learning from your students.

For your convenience, free teaching materials such as blank schedule forms, topic boards, small group schedules, data sheets, roles and responsibilities charts, routine lesson plan templates and visual supports are available online at www.autismclassroom.com . AutismClassroom.com also has a video/photo sharing component for teachers and para-professionals to get ideas for their classroom, an interactive message board for educators to discuss educational issues, and virtual consulting for classroom teams looking to enhance their current classroom's effectiveness. For parents, family members, caregivers and in-home support providers, AutismClasssroom.com offers two other book resources: How to Set Up a Work Area at Home for a Child with Autism and Functional Behavior Assessments & Behavior Intervention Plans. For more information about the books and resources, go to www.autismclassroom.com.

References

The following books and websites have been useful in creating this book. They are listed below:

Bondy, Andy & Frost, Lori (2002). A Picture's Worth: Pecs and Other Visual Communication Strategies in Autism. Woodbine House.

Bruce, Stephen & Gurdin, Lisa Selznick & Savage, Ron (2006). Strategies for Managing Challenging Behaviors of Students with Brain Injuries. Lash and Associates Publishing.

Cafiero, Joanne (2005). Meaningful Exchanges for People with Autism An Introduction to Augmentative and Alternative Communication. Woodbine House.

Downing, June & Bailey, Brent R. (1990) Sharing the Responsibility: Using a Transdisciplinary Team Approach to Enhance the Learning of Students With Severe Disabilities *Journal of Educational and Psychological Consultation*, 1, No. 3, 259-278.

Hodgdon, Linda (2001). Solving Behavior Problems in Autism: Improving Communication with Visual Strategies. Quirk Roberts Publishing.

Hodgdon, Linda (1995). Visual Strategies for Improving Communication: Practical Supports for School and Home. QuirkRoberts Publishing.

Linton, S. B. (2009). How to Set Up a Work Area at Home for a Child with Autism. AutismClassroom.com

McClannahan, Lynn & Krantz, Patricia (1999). Activity Schedules for Children With Autism: Teaching Independent Behavior. Woodbine House.

Moyes, Rebecca (2002). Addressing Challenging Behaviors in High Functioning Autism and Asperger's Syndrome. London: Jessica Kingsley Publishers Ltd.

Stock Kranowitz, Carol (2006). The Out-of-Sync Child: Recognizing and Coping with Sensory Processing Disorder. Penguin Group (USA).

www.autismclassroom.com
www.iancommunity.org
www.mayerjohnson.com
www.PBIS.org
www.polyxo.com
www.specialed.us/autism/assist/asst10.htm
www.teacch.com
www.usevisualstrategies.com

NOTES:

31883152R00048

Made in the USA
San Bernardino, CA
22 March 2016